JAMES S. BROCK

Morocco earthquake

Death toll, extent of damage, rescue efforts—Important facts you should know.

Contents

SECTION 1

Introduction

Morocco, a nation renowned for its fascinating past, breathtaking scenery, and vibrant culture, experienced a devastating earthquake that reverberated throughout its interior. This earthquake, one of the strongest in more than a century, devastated both rural villages nestled in the Atlas Mountains and the ancient city of Marrakech, leaving a trail of despair. In this in-depth article, we examine the effects of the earthquake in Morocco, current rescue operations, and difficulties faced by the affected communities.

Impact and magnitude

Unprecedented force was used to unleash the fury of the magnitude 6.8 earthquake, which occurred late on a fateful Friday night. Mountainsides collapsed, buildings shook, and it appeared as though the ground itself was convulsing. No part of Morocco remained untouched by the magnitude of this earthquake, which was felt not only in its immediate vicinity but also throughout the entire country. More than 800 lives were tragically lost, and as rescue teams fought against the clock, the death toll kept rising.

Impacted regions

This earthquake's epicenter was located high in the Atlas Mountains, about 70 kilometers south of the cosmopolitan city of Marrakech. The hardest hit area was this region, which is well-known for its rocky landscape, picturesque gorges, and idyllic lakes. The destruction that the earthquake caused in cities like Marrakech, Taroudant, and Chichaoua was a result of the tremors that echoed through the red-rock mountains, highlighting the disaster's wide- ranging effects.

Quick action and relief efforts

As the chaos subsided and the scope of the catastrophe became clear, Morocco's law enforcement and aid personnel acted quickly. The affected area was the focus of a coordinated national and international effort. Soldiers, ambulances, and rescue teams all showed up to help with emergency response. Residents were given food and water, and teams toiled nonstop to clear the mountain roads that had become perilous barriers due to the boulders that littered them.

Long-TermHealing

While immediate relief efforts met urgent needs and gave survivors vital assistance, the road to recovery was difficult and drawn out. The issue of shelter loomed large as the country struggled to comprehend the tragedy's scope, and the threat of impending rain made the situation even worse. The effects of the earthquake on housing and essential services, as well as infrastructure, presented serious difficulties for the affected communities.

Following this catastrophe, Morocco is faced with the enormous task of rebuilding destroyed communities and lives. Although it will take some time for the earthquake's wounds to heal, the Moroccan people's fortitude and tenacity will undoubtedly show in the face of hardship. The world looks on sympathetically as the country begins its path to recovery and extends a helping hand to a nation renowned for its beauty, culture, and resilient spirit.

SECTION 2

Humanitarian Support and Aid

As a result of the devastating earthquake that struck Morocco, a great deal of property and human life has been lost. It is impossible to overstate the significance of humanitarian assistance and support in the wake of this natural disaster. This article explores the extensive humanitarian response and the crucial role that different organizations, governments, and volunteers played in providing those affected with immediate relief and assistance.

A Summary of Aid Agencies

Following the earthquake, many organizations came together to offer assistance and support. Governments, regional and global organizations, and even unpaid volunteers were among them. The military and the Moroccan government collaborated to an important extent to mobilize personnel and assets for rescue and relief operations. Local charities and community groups intervened as well to provide support at the grassroots level.

Governmental and global responses

Governments from all over the world responded internationally after the earthquake in Morocco. Spain, Qatar, the United Arab Emirates, Britain, and other nations offered assistance in the form of financial aid, medical supplies, and search and rescue teams. These coordinated efforts served as an example of how the world comes together in times of need. Nations united despite their political differences to aid a struggling neighboring country.

Red Cross and other organizations' roles

Humanitarian efforts were led by the International Federation of Red Cross and Red Crescent Societies (IFRC). They quickly released $1.1 million to support the relief efforts of the Moroccan Red Crescent from their Disaster Response Emergency Fund. With the help of its committed volunteers, the Moroccan Red Crescent worked tirelessly to provide displaced families with aid, healthcare, and shelter.

Issues and Future Assistance

Even though there has been a lot of progress in providing emergency relief, there are still obstacles to overcome on the road to recovery. There are still many areas that have an urgent need for shelter, food, clean water, and medical supplies. The affected communities must undertake the difficult task of reconstructing their infrastructure, homes, and way of life. It is also crucial to offer survivors of trauma psychological support and trauma counseling.

Future support from the international community for Morocco's efforts at long-term recovery is essential. Reconstruction and rehabilitation will necessitate ongoing financial support, technical know-how, and cooperation between authorities, groups, and neighborhood groups. To lessen the effects of upcoming earthquakes, disaster preparedness, and risk reduction measures must also be strengthened.

SECTION 3

Local Effects and Community Reaction to the Moroccan Earthquake

The devastating earthquake that hit Morocco has permanently changed the lives of the locals in the affected areas. Numerous Moroccans' lives were forever altered as the ground shook and structures collapsed. This article explores the heartbreaking tales coming out of the disaster's epicenter, highlighting the fortitude of the affected communities and the crucial role local government and aid agencies played.

Tales from the Affected Regions

High in the Atlas Mountains, where the earthquake's epicenter was located, were picturesque villages that had, up until that fateful night, been relatively calm. These tranquil settings were transformed into scenes of devastation after the catastrophe. For instance, Tafeghaghte residents recall the terrifying moments when their homes collapsed, taking many lives in the process. As they cope with grief and trauma, survivors experience an indescribable emotional toll.

Toll of Death and Injury

This earthquake has cost an incredible number of lives. Morocco is mourning its losses after the most recent count revealed more than 2,800 fatalities. The suffering is evident in small towns like Tafeghaghte, where more than half the population died. Families have been shattered, and this tragedy will leave scars that last for generations.

Thousands of people were hurt, and their road to recovery will be difficult. As they work to give aid and support to those in need, hospitals and medical teams are overburdened. As volunteers and local healthcare professionals work tirelessly to save lives, it is a testament to human solidarity.

Community Needs Right Away

The immediate needs of the affected communities became clear as the aftershocks and dust settled. Nobody had a place to live, or access to clean water, or electricity. Food supplies were running low, and the threat of disease outbreaks was very real. Locals came together, pooling their remaining resources, demonstrating Morocco's tenacious spirit.

The Function of Local Governments

The Moroccan government quickly organized resources to address the crisis. Coordination of the rescue and relief operations was greatly helped by local authorities. But even the best-prepared response teams were unable to handle the disaster's scope. Getting around damaged infrastructure and helping isolated mountain villages were difficult.

Construction and Rehabilitation

Thoughts are already turning to the enormous task of rebuilding, even though the immediate priority is still on saving lives and providing relief. It's a process that will take a lot of time and money. The Moroccan government is dedicated to assisting communities in rebuilding their homes, infrastructure, and lives with the assistance of international partners.

In conclusion, the earthquake in Morocco has had a devastating impact on the affected areas, but it has also highlighted the remarkable fortitude and resilience of the Moroccan people. The tales that are coming out of the disaster area are examples of human comradery and the unwavering will to overcome obstacles and rebuild. The international community is keeping an eye on the recovery efforts and is prepared to help Morocco on its path to recovery and restoration.

SECTION 4

Marrakech's importance

The "Red City," also known as Marrakech, occupies a special place in Moroccan history and culture. Due to its designation as a UNESCO World Heritage site, its significance transcends national boundaries. The region's heritage has been permanently impacted by the city's lengthy history, which spans more than a thousand years.

Marrakech earthquake damage

That fateful day's earthquake in Morocco sent shockwaves through Marrakech, shaking the city's historic structures and old walls. The damage was sub- stantial even though it wasn't as bad as in some of the more remote rural areas closer to the epicenter. The Koutoubia Mosque was one of many famous buildings that was damaged by the earthquake.

Impact of Culture and Heritage

It is impossible to overstate the earthquake's effects on Marrakech's cultural and historical heritage. The vibrant souls, intricately carved palaces, and historic medina of Marrakech are well-known attractions. These works of architecture not only helped to define the city but also drew visitors and academics from all over the world. The earthquake posed a threat to centuries of art and history.

Preservation Initiatives

After the earthquake, preservation initiatives got underway. To evaluate the damage and create plans for restoration and reconstruction, government agencies, NGOs, and international organizations worked together. Together with local experts, preservationists and architects from all over the world came up with a plan to protect Marrakech's cultural treasures.

The Heritage of Marrakech's Future

While the earthquake significantly damaged Marrakech's heritage, it also sparked discussions about the city's future preservation efforts. Authorities and specialists debated how to strike a balance between the need for modern development and the desire to preserve the city's historic identity. Initiatives were started to make sure that Marrakech's architectural integrity was preserved during reconstruction.

The strength of the people of Marrakech and the assistance of the international community have brought the city hope. The entire world watches as Marrakech works to rebuild not only its physical infrastructure but also its identity as a protector of Morocco's past and a sign of its future.

The earthquake that shook Marrakech served as a stark reminder of the fine line that must be drawn between upholding tradition and welcoming change. It is evidence of the resilient character of a city that, in the face of nature's destructive forces, continues to hold on to its rich past. Marrakech, with its vivid hues and intricate patterns, continues to be a representation of tenacity and a living example of how heritage shapes our world.

SECTION 5

Earthquake History in Morocco

It's critical to comprehend Morocco's seismic history before moving on to a global perspective. Morocco has experienced earthquakes throughout its history, and the most recent one was among the strongest in more than a century. For evaluating the impact and preparedness steps taken in the wake of such a significant event, the historical context is essential.

Compared to Other Earthquakes Around the World

Comparing the Moroccan earthquake to other significant seismic events worldwide is one of the first steps in comprehending the implications of the earthquake. We can find patterns and trends that offer useful insights for future disaster preparedness by comparing and contrasting the earthquakes in Morocco with those in other regions.

Standards for Construction and Buildings

The quality of a building's construction and building codes are crucial factors in determining how much damage an earthquake will cause. This section will look at how Morocco's construction standards fared during the earthquake and make comparisons to global norms. To identify weak points and potential areas for development, evaluating building practices across various regions is essential.

Disaster Prevention and Preparedness

Any response to a seismic event should focus first and foremost on disaster preparedness. We'll compare Morocco's preparation efforts to those in other earthquake-prone areas. Evaluations of early warning systems, evacuation strategies, and the efficiency of emergency response teams are all part of this process. Nations all over the world can improve their preparedness efforts by taking lessons from both successes and failures.

Observations and Lessons for Future Earthquakes

This article's final section will concentrate on the global applications of the lessons discovered from the earthquake in Morocco. Each seismic event offers a chance to improve strategies and policies in the ongoing process of earthquake preparedness. We'll talk about how crucial it is for nations to work together to share information and best practices to lessen the effects of earthquakes in the future.

Conclusion

The earthquake in Morocco has irreparably changed the country, but it also has a wealth of lessons for the entire world. We can all work together to lessen the destruction brought on by earthquakes in the future by analyzing this seismic event in the context of global earthquake preparedness. The world is committed to a safer and more resilient future in the face of natural disasters and is watching and learning as Morocco continues its journey toward recovery and reconstruction.